My Automobile Dealership

A true story.

Grace LaJoy
Henderson, PhD

Inspirations by Grace LaJoy
Raymore, MO
www.gracelajoy.com
poetry@gracelajoy.com

Cover by Grace LaJoy Henderson

MY AUTOMOBILE DEALERSHIP
Copyright © 2010 by Grace LaJoy Henderson
Published by Inspirations by Grace LaJoy
Raymore, MO 64083
www.gracelajoy.com

ISBN: 978-0-9829404-0-2

All rights reserved. No portion of this book may be copied, reproduced or transmitted in any form without prior written permission from the publisher.

Printed in the United States of America

Foreword

For so long, automobile dealerships and their salespersons have been looked upon as people who play sales number games in order to sell vehicles. But, they have another side to them that is not always readily seen by vehicle buyers. A sincere side that understands that their continued growth depends on their commitment to display honest, loyalty and fair treatment to every person. This includes doing what is best for those who depend on them for quality vehicles and service.

When the motives of automobile sales industry are questioned, it results in a barrier of distrust. When this type of barrier has been built, it can only be broken by instilling trust into those who have been affected.

Through, MY AUTOMOBILE DEALERSHIP, Dr. Grace LaJoy sets out to break that barrier by sharing her true, inspirational story of how she benefited from the helpful and caring side of her automobile dealership. Her story shows that while sales are important, automobile salespersons also have a genuine concern for helping individuals and families chose a vehicle that fits their needs.

My Automobile Dealership   Grace LaJoy Henderson, PhD

My Automobile Dealership   Grace LaJoy Henderson, PhD

Recently, I began thinking about the personal road I've traveled during my life. I came from being a young mother to a successful author and speaker. As I thought about the many resources that have carried me through life, my automobile dealership came to mind again and again – sales, service *and* credit. Over the years I have found my dealership vehicles to be dependable, durable and safe.

Going back more than twenty-five years, my automobile dealership is in the picture.

My father taught me to always buy, and have my car serviced and repaired, at a dealership. He would always say, "A vehicle does not have to break down after so many years; it can last a lifetime if you take care of it." He taught me that dealerships offered the best terms and service on automobile loans.

Leaning on everything my father taught me, I went to a dealership when I was ready to purchase my first car. I had just graduated from high school, had a part-time job, and enough money for a large down payment. The salesman helped me chose a car that was appropriate, yet affordable for me.

My Automobile Dealership   Grace LaJoy Henderson, PhD

After a little bit of negotiation, we purchased the car. With help from the salesman, I ended up with an automobile loan and a payment I could afford. My automobile dealership even helped me obtain the car insurance I needed!

After driving my first car for about four years, I decided to trade it in for a newer model. This time I did not have money for a down payment. I did not have sufficient credit to get the loan amount I needed. But, I *did* have a plan.

I had a great aunt who had excellent credit. She and I went to the automobile dealership hoping they would let her co-sign for my loan. The salesman collected my financial information...then he collected hers. She had every credit card that a person could have.

The salesman submitted our credit application while we waited. Soon he was back and told us what we already knew -- my great aunt had excellent credit. Then he told me something I was happy to hear -- the automobile loan was approved. With his help, I drove off the lot with a car that fit my needs!

My Automobile Dealership Grace LaJoy Henderson, PhD

My automobile dealership sells only quality vehicles. They offer superior service as well. I have never experienced major mechanical problems with cars purchased from my dealership. But, whenever any of my vehicles needed to be serviced, they were always there with a friendly helping hand.

Not only has my automobile dealership been a benefit to me, they have helped me to help my children. Because of the excellent quality of vehicles they sell, and the great automotive service they provide, I was able to keep one of my cars in the family for several years, passing it down to my son.

When my daughter was ready to buy her first car, we decided to buy from an individual in our town. The car looked clean, but, we were concerned because it had high mileage. I needed to be sure that the car was reliable.

So, before we paid for the car, I took it to my car dealership and had it inspected. After about one hour, the serviceman came to the lobby and told me the car was in excellent condition and that it had been well cared for. He assured me my daughter would be safe in it! Once again, my automobile dealership came through for me!

My Automobile Dealership   Grace LaJoy Henderson, PhD

When my daughter was able to afford a newer vehicle, we went to our local automobile dealership, where we found our best deal.

She did not have a down payment, nor did she have established credit. So, the salesman assisted me in the process of co-signing for her loan …and it was approved!

While driving one day, my daughter got into an accident in which her new car was totaled! Being in college at the time, she had become dependent on her car to get her to class. So, I traveled to her college campus, which was two hours away, and brought her home so we could take care of some business from the wrecked car and find her a new one. We needed to find it within a few hours because she needed to drive back to college so she would not miss class the next morning.

By then, I had truly become aware that my automobile dealership had great cars and reasonable prices. So, I took her directly there!

This time, she had a large down payment and had some credit established. So, the salesman assisted her in filling out a loan application. He helped us to determine whether to request the loan in my daughter's name only, or if I should co-sign for her.

Within minutes, the application was approved while we waited. I know salesmen want the sale to go through – they work on commission. But, this salesman seemed to have a genuine concern for my daughter getting back to her college campus.

My daughter drove that car back and forth to college many times. She drove it to her summer camp sites where she was a camp counselor for children. She has even driven to other states to visit friends.

The car has not had *any* mechanical problems at all. My daughter has since graduated from college with a Master's degree in Social Work. So, she now uses her car to help secure emergency, temporary and permanent shelter, for children in foster care.

My automobile dealership assisted me. They also helped me to help my children. Now they are helping my child help *other* children.

I wonder sometimes if automobile dealers ever think about all the people who drive the vehicles they sell and service. Not just when they are new and shiny and have a new car smell. But, years later those same vehicles are still safe and reliable.

Over the past twenty five years, I have purchased several cars through my automobile dealership. From being a young mother to becoming a successful author and speaker, my automobile dealership has helped me secure the transportation I needed. They also ensured my cars were properly serviced and safe for the road. More importantly, my automobile dealership has assisted me with obtaining the *finances* to have reliable, dependable transportation.

I often think about the long road I have traveled during my life. I think about the people at my automobile dealership – those who sold and serviced the cars and those who helped me with financing the cars – and I am grateful.

Can you afford to buy, or save for, a car?
This financial worksheet will help you determine.

Income	
	Amount ($)
Wages/Salary	
Interest	
Dividends	
Other Income	
Total Income	
Expenses	
	Amount ($)
Mortgage/Rent	
Food/Drink	
Electricity	
Gas	
Water/Sewer	
Phone	
Cable	
Credit Card	
Recreation	
Memberships	
Toiletries	
Other Expenses	
Total Expenses	
Total Income – Total Expenses	

Note: If your total income minus your total expenses results in a positive amount, you may be able to afford a car payment or to save for a car. If you desire a car loan, your dealership salesperson can help to determine if you qualify for credit. If you already have a car and considering trading it for a newer vehicle, your dealership salesperson can also help you determine the value of your trade-in.

Here are thirteen (13) important questions to ask when considering a car loan?

What is the state sales tax rate?

What is the selling price of the car?

What is the total amount of the sales tax?

Is there a rebate?

Is a down payment needed? If so, how much?

What is the value of my trade-in?

How much money needs to be borrowed?

How many months is the loan?

What is the interest rate/annual percentage rate?

What is the total amount of interest to be paid on the loan?

What is the monthly payment amount?

What is the total cost of the loan, including interest?

What is the total cost of the car, including taxes, rebate, and interest?

Notes

Notes

Notes

Notes

Notes

Notes

Notes

ABOUT THE AUTHOR

Dr. Grace LaJoy Henderson was born in Kalamazoo, Michigan a small town just outside of Grand Rapids, Michigan on November 22, 1966. She went into foster care in Kansas City, Missouri when she was seven years old and remained in foster care until age ten. Before foster care, she attended C.A. Franklin Elementary School in Kansas City, Missouri. While in foster care, she attended J.S. Chick Elementary School. After foster care, she lived in Charlotte, North Carolina and attended Hidden Valley Elementary, Ransom Junior High and West Charlotte High schools. She began her senior year at Westport High School in Kansas City, Missouri. After graduation, she attended Penn Valley Community College in Kansas City, Missouri where she eventually received an Associates of Science degree in Office Management. She received a Bachelor's degree in Social Psychology from Park College, in Kansas City, Missouri and a PhD from Faith Bible College in Independence, Missouri. She has professional and volunteer experience working with youth and families.

Dr. LaJoy has appeared in local and national news including Fox-4 news and TBN's Praise the Lord program. She has been featured in the Kansas City Star, The Star Herald – Belton Missouri, and the Independence Examiner just to name a few newspapers. She is currently a speaker for Stonecroft International Ministries. She speaks and reads poetry at churches and conducts author visits at schools predominately in the Kansas City Metropolitan and surrounding areas. She conducts an annual workshop for writers and aspiring authors. She has even received an endorsement from Motivational Speaker, Les Brown.

She has self-published a total of seventeen books since January of 2003. Her latest book is entitled, "A Gifted Child in Foster Care: A Story of Resilience", which comes with a matching Teacher's Guide and Student Workbook. Her mission is to change the way children are viewed who live in diverse situations, such as foster care; and to magnify the fact that all children have a gift and the ability to be successful regardless of their background or circumstances.

www.ingramcontent.com/pod-product-compliance
Lightning Source LLC
Chambersburg PA
CBHW071848290426
44109CB00017B/1971